I0813264

THE BELLA VISTA

POEMS

EMMA RUTH RUNDLE

THE UNNAMED PRESS
LOS ANGELES, CA

AN UNNAMED PRESS BOOK

Published in North America by the Unnamed Press.

www.unnamedpress.com

Unnamed Press and the colophon are registered trademarks of Unnamed Media LLC.

Hardcover ISBN: 978-1-961884-32-8
Ebook ISBN: 978-1-961884-20-5

LCCN: 2024947591

Cover photograph by Ebru Yildiz
Cover design and typeset by Jaya Nicely

Manufactured in the United States of America

Distributed by Publishers Group West

First Edition

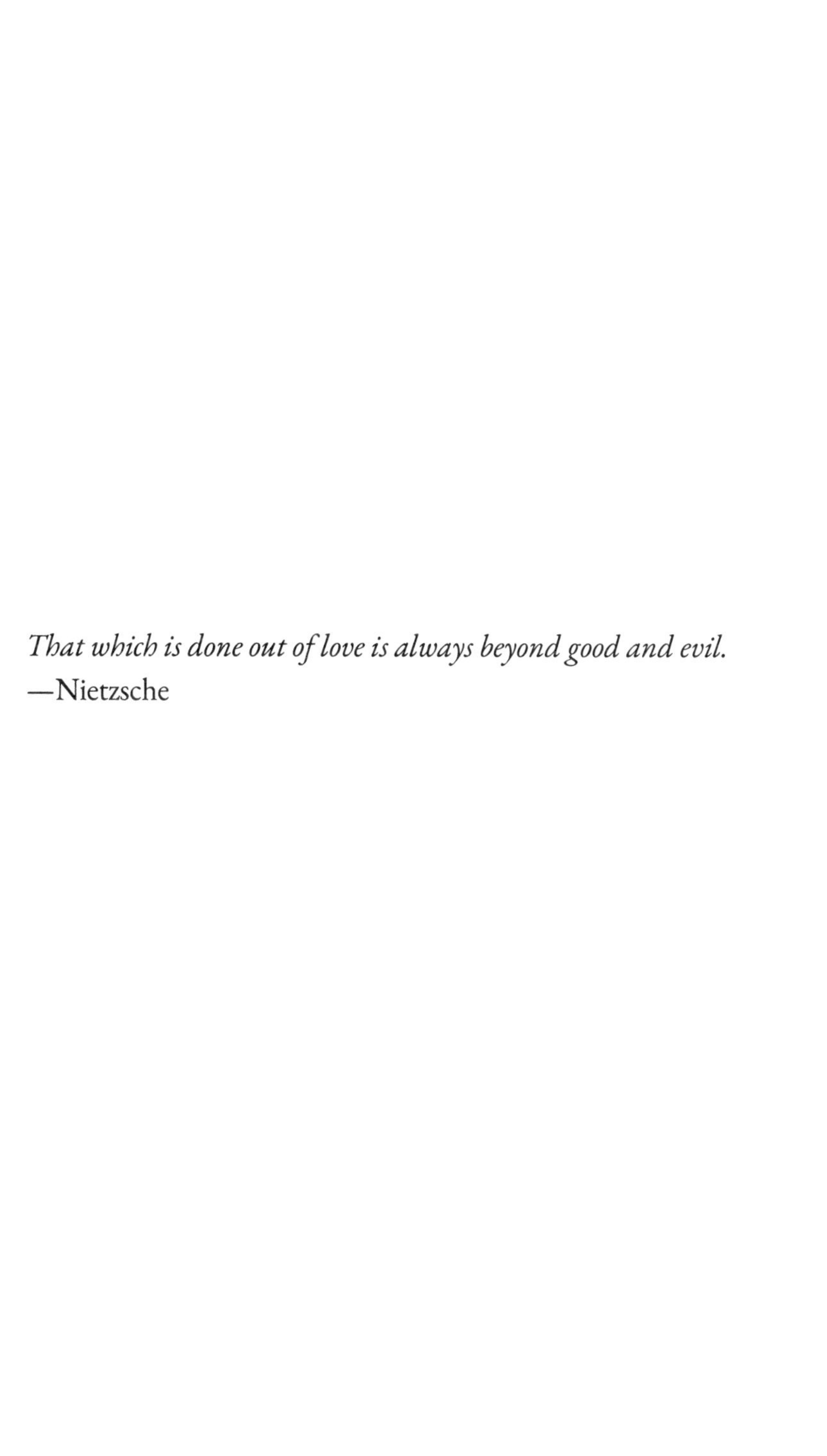

That which is done out of love is always beyond good and evil.
—Nietzsche

CONTENTS

THE BELLA VISTA

rip up this book, my love
i wrote it for you
so that
crumpled pages of refuse worthy
thinking might lift from the floor and bloom
peony and chrysanthemum
rightfully placed upon your shoulders.
words and thoughts aren't enough.
they aren't even close to right.
i wish i'd never known any language at all
other than the giving of simple gifts.

THE BELLA VISTA

BACI

darkness is just darkness.

POEM FROM AN UNSENT POSTCARD

There is nothing to say
which is original of our love
For ours is the origin of all things
My rib returned to your welcoming cage
Is a swallow, safe and contented
Who will sing then

And your heart finally made whole
At Maat's great scale
Does a feather only weigh
And permits you back into heaven
And to your place among the stars
The origin of all things

POEM FROM A POSTCARD WHICH I DID SEND

I recall you
In dim visions
With vivid shoots
Of Strawberry Moons
Watering mothers keep and
Bless you, The Son of the Moon!
The sole sweller of my tides

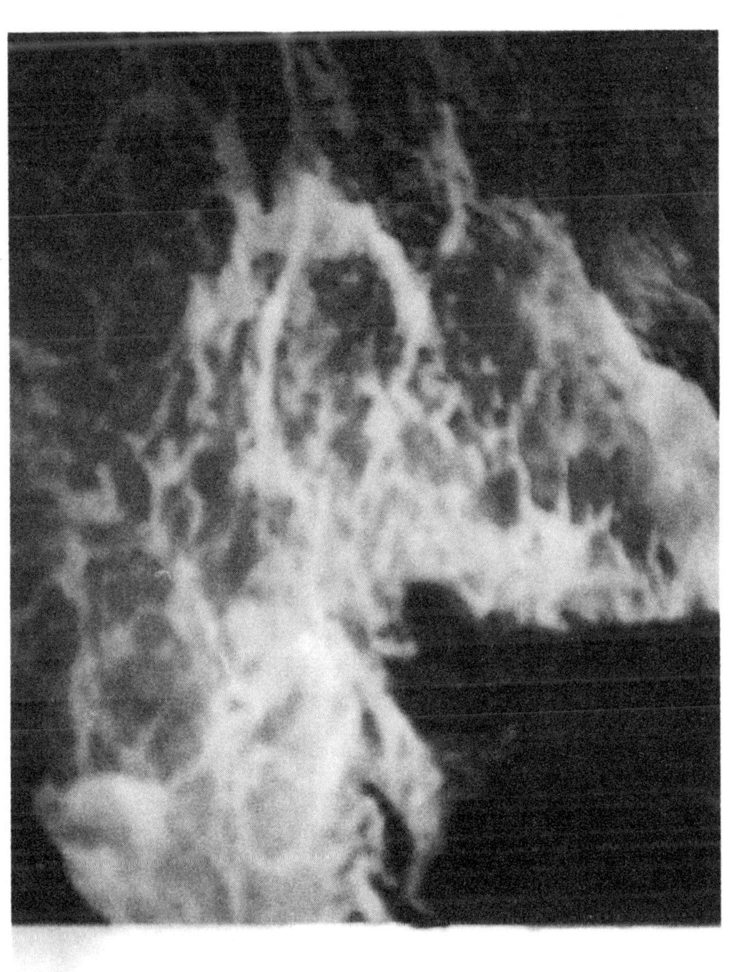

LEIRIAN

Full of swords like that etching of
the wounded man.
From out to in
and at angles.
Twisting in a heated mess.
Leaves on this Portuguese tree
furl inward
away from the anguishing swelter.
Making their own small shade
in each green sheet bending.
Seeking a relief
that cannot come by action.
But only in waiting out the day
and its searing shards.

I READ TOO MUCH HEMINGWAY

I am increased
In flesh that is young and flooded.
The Lord of All Things was weeping
And washed us generously.
With abundance, Dear One You Are Loved.

Lie, restore with me
That I may increase you.
Even with shyness,
quiet singing.

There is a perfect vessel
in shallow of your sternum
where the rapeseed of our shame
we press into an oil
and curl wick there.

A lamp there
lights The Son of the Moon
so I can see him from great distance.
Soon I will lay on you
and sew into your skin
the red threads of chosen family.

Before you are burned away
Before ash can reclaim our small purchase.
And the lovers are increased
In the origin flood
In arcing showers of many springtimes
Joyful tears and sweated labors

In this work
We are washed
And sown and increased
Our destination is an unburdened one
In us, an arable land

HELIUM VELLUM

Good night me.
Tuck me in.
I'm not asking.

Good knights we think on and become queer,
lusting after The Archangel's blade
and his foe

"*Think about,*" I used to call it,
the profane touching of the self.

Nothing changes in the needs of a person
who stopped aging at their first drink
and forever; Innocent but Temperamental

The Eternal Child
A pickled/wet Specimen
An Incorruptible Infanta

Indeed under duress
at the drop of a junked-up mommy.

Hitting the floor,
it's genetic...

Now any sudden thud sends us swifting
to the Ativan dispensary
Which is always at hand.
Never looking for a fight.

Dumbo's Magic Feather
The Red Balloon
James's Giant Peach

Other prescriptions for flight suggest one should just:

think happy thoughts...

PALOMA

Wind blows my dove-shaped kite into the sun.
quickening away
the string intermittently burns my tensioning finger.
R.P. doesn't let me look anywhere towards the light

On Father's blindness.
On Father's bullets and unspooled intestines

our surgeries and stolen organs sailing upward on sinews
like red ribbons snaking high in the desert scirocco

Also, I taped over its eyes and feet with white duct tape.

I was hoping to hide
The fact that she is, in truth,
only an ugly seagull

blinding her as we are blinded
binding her as we are bound

This pinioned kite.

I just wanted to see something pure
gliding upwards
Out of the dirt
Into the sky
Out from the stark interior
Into the canopic jars of the cloudless beyond.

To lessen the gravity of our blackening brio
The velocity of escape is 7 miles a second
In My Child Heart.
It's too heavy anyway—

Only now and then does she make it
high enough to meet the sun

And I can't see that anyway—
My back is always turned to you
My father's blindness is always ahead
In shadow, anyway—

I thought I glimpsed
the holy spirit

ON THE TARMAC AT PSP

My joy lives in you, my arable land.
Even living out in the desert
You stay liquid.
You say your river flows in two directions at
once I asked if you meant

Like an escalator?

I meant to say "like two"
Like in a shopping mall.
Or like the moving walkways in an airport
Those metal stairs and flowing belts
seem to always carry me farther from your person
Our secret wounds become not secret
and both repel and heal us

When we are separated
The fresh skin is again sloughed
and so our nakedness is a risk.
All this sloughing hopes to reveal us
lasting as new babes
All the drinking of you hopes
to slake the need of love
All the drinks of a lifetime cannot slake that need
and the addict's soul is a sieve
which cannot hold you
and cannot hold her liquor
That was then.

BACI

the 27 club are alive and well and singing
people don't really kill themselves over things like that
but i read you can die of a broken heart

WINTER GARDEN

I can't write about Borges
and blindness
and the beauty of
the twilight of the senses.
Because I'm not over Burroughs
and burdens
and intimate guns pointed
in the winter garden.

Between the branches
The leafless tree of family
The greenless wreath of bornness
The splintering body of ancestry
The addled hands of mothers
The distant hands of fathers
The violent nature of our being here.
The violent nature of love.

AFTER THAT UNBEARABLY COLD CHURCH SHOW IN EASTERN EUROPE, THE ONE A CAT CAME TO

Unexpectedly you sent me flowers.
From across the world and time,
you gathered up species,
like a Victorian,
from pages and paintings.
With no notice or reason
you loved me again today.
Plying my not-so-reluctant girl
from her bitterly hidden slippers
back into blushing gardens.
No amount of weeks
lived in an ice house
improved her resolve
To remain alone again.

You harvested from the desert sky
cut flowers, impossible, and to Zephyr handed leaf

rain

So that pages of pressed tulips and petals

over what was the Soviet Union

upon leaf Fragments of forbidden tomes

a volcanic lush blown

purposeful ash and ember

where snow, only a day before,

was drifting down

with great uncertainty

When I cried in the decrepit palatial hotel
because I really knew you couldn't sow anything for me.

Then overnight springtime.
I'll never understand you.

THE STARMAKER

AFTER REMEDIOS VARO

Sweet boy
Unsure man
Line of a man
The most hidden being
You've not yet been discovered
Not even unto yourself
What thoughts are you trying to keep out
When you build your pillow fortress
and lord in the citadel of sleeplessness?
Whose little army will not let you rest?
The lord god?
The father god?
The doings of men who've done and been done to them
as children, as brothers, as sons?
Three generations of war?
An old song you once loved and are now tortured by
drowning the unsavory dreamer?
Or the fear of wakening again to the faithless
Destroyer-of-Worlds world in which we really live?

I never want to waken.

As lovers, only sometimes,
our eyes meet in the mourning bed
And I well up because of your indescribables—
the directness to your lineage of sorrows
and so short-lived a moment it is.

You do not hold my gaze
but you will hold my hand

I am waiting at the gate
I am sitting at the edge of the water there
In case the poet does descend
When the starmaker is free and the moon is fed
In case you might make the crossing
unburdened and without fear of me

I have stilled the morning chorus
I've warned the birds not to sing
I do not eat but drink
on silence and lacrimosa
I open my mouth to become the vessel of Nothingness
And cast the vacuum, like a long-held note of shadow, all around your tower.

No creature here stirs
No creature here dares stir
That we may behold you, most rare one
My dweller on the threshold.

BACI

Art will require sacrifices
you really can't
imagine
when you first
pick up her tools
and summon the unseen

CAMPANILE

We stood in the window to look out over the pits next to Parkview.
A city of devouring urges corrupting elsewhere.

You'd just offered me the right to all the carnations.
Two neonate buddings of carefree circumstance.

You asked if I knew your last name.
I lied and shook my head no.
You said some eastern angel had fallen—

—to give you that name.
Three generations of war.
Three degrees from god.

You've always had that wooden heart
Hanging around your neck.
A sailboat. An eye. The water.

You want to send me out
into the world in that little boat.
Just a mouse, me.

I ask you to recharge its powers
by holding it to your forehead
where I'd kiss you if you were my child.

Looking at the window,
I see your father's damage reflected in your posture
and his ████████████ in your face.
REDACTED

ROSE WINDOW

pomegranates
seed
the
afternoon
many
mini
moons
opalesce
your
affections
childless
in
the
headwaters
the
riverspring
the
unburdened
the
reborn
in
gilded
cups
of
stars
and
semen

ROSE WINDOW WITH FIVE OF COINS

Sour and scaled aperture of us obdurates
Such misery and too twisted faces
Winter of the mourning
Wife of the unyielding darkened day
Meals from a can repeating
It’s not a relapse because I didn’t drink
Everything prescribed
I don’t play music
I have no music to play
Where joy is living as a leper
I will never sing again

A DREAM I FALL INTO LYING NEXT TO YOU

tree farm. chicken farm.
i know it was Ivan's dream
of spilling apple carts at the water's edge
that unsettled the mind, unsettled the day

herds cracked open the nights.
and if they were ever to fall into a silence
rain then nailing hard on that rural tin roof
bbs streaming down from daddy's toy gun

the woman was junk-sick and would moan too.
she was lonely and deeply heart-wounded.
the kind we call all too broken.
and her joints hurt her badly.

she would lie, like a woman twice her age, for days
on a deathbed-like place in a blue tin can
to see if facing the North Star might ease
that woe become her.

lowing in the late morning.
mommy is still
tiny saviors behind the wall
beating dirge of the sick that sleeps

sucking pop sounds finally opening
little not yet women
attached to the last of the frozen breads
hope eats the daily horizon.

tomorrow another country.
tonight another war.

My mind is twisted
a tear slid down a bread-filled cheek.
The mind inside the body,
matter-of-fact-like.

keep silent in this house.
twenty toes tucked into a child bride's shoes.
little lords of pleasure perform
to entertain the dead bedder,
to see her smile from her opium cloisters,
dance with quick neat feet

mommy would laugh so hard until something in her would
twist out a She-Saturn, ready to devour

and the girls would cry and run
and hide and become wild
out through slammed doors
into the muddy trenches of neglected youth.

let out of the car miles from home one night.
stumbling down the highway at dusk
in royal heels no babes should wear
twin Anastasias exiled on the gravel shoulder.

filth sucks Innocence right off Her feet
naked and crossing The Sadness
the last of the bread.
the last of the highway.

Poison weeds the golden fields,
The Kingdom Have Come
losing teeth and growing new ones
losing weight but growing wings

children sometimes dream they have awakened
and sometimes waking children force themselves back into dream.

mounted daughters crashing houses
sleeping mothers falling into a crack under the bed.
mirror that marks the edge of reality.
a time unkind and all Christina's World.

those white shoes.
those bare feet.
milk-skinned children.
born of skimmed-milk women

no chickenshit spirits here.
no bad luck in this mirror breaking.
apples and Christmas trees
and fully baked bread.

"run to me my girls!"
the light of some midsummer wheat sheafed
and heaved the girls at speed
up to the High Heavens.

I wake up crying and hope you don't notice
I know you're not sleeping.

MOLESKINE KNOCKOFFS

I've given up on paper and little notebooks
The ones you gifted me shall be the last to return from foreign shores
Empty souvenirs of their wordless owner's wordlessness
The last to hit a burn pile

See, you've drunk up all the language.
Your vocation hoards the remnants and sparse syntax
So that I have no *where* from which to begin a line
And am corralled by uncertain phrases

But to call to you—that's still clear and as incorruptible
As the first formed vowel in the primordial moths mum
Everything after a name is lost to the poet's collection
Jangling around like Scrabble pieces in your unsentimental machine

From a couplet turned fragment
Ambling scribbling taping blindly with a bloody grin
Back on foreign shores,
He's not yet vacuumed the landscape of its languages here

The giant laureate himself never crossed the seas
And so I'm gathering again in this Eden
And free to sing from outside the formless place
Of that man's wake

Every narcissus a new turn of phrase
Every flight a fresh metaphor
Restore my tooth and pen
In the eruption of this nubile season

FLAYED AS ANYTHING THAT HATES

Nonspecific white sheets
Pile indifferently over your prayer box
You were gaunt even in youth
But now, water can only reach you
by crooked straw

Desert poet,
Did you bury the mountain?
Did you ever split your river?
Did you "let love in"?
Did you write a perfect line?
Or did that thief, apprehension,
exchange the brief fruits of summer
for your safety named regret
I hope you named her thusly

Sick in Geneva
Imagining you in your future fading age
Execrating you in all your tenses
Willing you to trials as I am tested
As no food passes my lips
As water only reaches crooked me by straw
As I fail to write a perfect line
Am shallower under indifferent sheets
And let that hustler-cum-fear
Shake me down
for all the brief hopes I had saved up to give you
in the form of a summer fruit...
hmmmmm...hmmmm...hm
Non, je ne regrette rien...
hmmmmm...hmmmm...hm

AT THE TOMB OF SAINT FRANCIS

At the tomb of Saint Francis
I knelt down and prayed for you
I bought a long white candle of offering
and gripped it with each finger.
With the letters of your name
I did mark the wax
so god would be certain
this one burning was yours.
And dropped it from one basket
into another.

closer to the tomb, I wept.
behind the crosshatched iron plaits, the stones,
hands stacked and crammed together,
immured the sainted corpse.

Makes you wonder if they are trying to keep him in
rather than the pious out.
Or if there's really anything inside at all.
And if we visit spirituality like a zoo...

"Where there is hatred"
What can you sow from this prison?

There's a millennial up for sainthood
whose miracle is a healed liver.
I pray now for your liver
and run my mind over the shuddering childlike sleeper
of your revealing.

an innocent boy
pulling doves from the white hole in the night
called Moon
I'd rewrite it all and hold you up
to that father sky you cry out for
to see all the little sparrows
break free from your joyous body,

ascending,
effulgent.
In Assisi, the rain lashes my descent

A flagellation
A pilgrimage

I will not seek to be consoled
I will not seek to be loved

GOODBYE HORSES

I

"I wrote about you"...

...my stomach sank in Strasbourg
...not again

A man I trust
has taken
to the page
the song
the image

exposing
my nectars
my interiors
and melodies

Entering
hotel rooms
uninvited
persons
half-mes

half-meats
uphill pill
person drunk
downright
desperate

But I Can't Quite Call It
████████████████ REDACTED

II

I imagine you as Buffalo Bill, the fictitious serial killer,
in his lair, held together by the skins of
the women he both loathed and coveted

"I wrote about you today"...

the fabrics of my confidence
my red robes even
Which I hang in my apartments, most private

trophy me
capture my essence
or try it on
pocket its perfumes
finger tip the violets
little violations

it's always to exalt you
they will surely claim

and a small gem of Innocence is plucked from Her shell.
Pearls are not of infinite manufacture

Love is a cruel jeweler setting
the diminishing stones
in an ever-dwindling Matryoshka
of diadems arranged by size;
dignity, humanity, womanhood, girlhood,
My ability to remain both vulnerable and intact

—my perseverance—

III

During working hours I volunteer woundings
and reveal in detail, or sometimes veiled frame/case—
I tell and for-sale myself as is necessary.

In the dolorous mines, inky pasts are
dragged up through Tartarus's pitch.
Down where mother floated sisters along that river.
Not ever making it to that place you described...

that you quoted from a poem about...
Some "mythic, liminal entrance to the above ground"
it was out of our hell, anyway.

Darkness is just darkness, they say
You say it's an easy pull

But on La Brea, sisters saw some
mother succumbing to the black lake
and did try the toy plungers to test
the resistance of its viscosity.
Tar

In some ways, a peddler of sadness
In others, a clown
but it's *mine* to sell or send in

delude the giver into allowing gone.
and they call it a *gift*

IV

Lucy looked great in his white suit dripping
with ungodly soilings at the ankles
and *HE* never needed shoes

to glide, like a shadow Jesus,
right over the dark waters of LA.

I wish to lovc a man and to hold him close
that he might also love and hold me
and see the little girl who simply seeks shelter—

struck with an iron ball and in need of help
in plunging off its weight.
Not just *needy.*
That someday, someone might come, without motive,
and just say
it's easy
To defy the gravity of the past—
in possession of no hidden shears with which to snip
fair hair or tender hem
with no need of recompense, he would come.

V

But this isn't the nature of us
and even as I vowed to carry you, little boy,
over your inked river,
I am not so righteous,

and when I see you as the betrayer,
I'll drop you into vitriol and shame
to send you down the very same
ebbing water of my own sulfuric baptism.
I'll place each of you in the corner
of words of song and of image.
I'll contain you on the page
and make you small when any audience gathers.

That is my power.
That is my design.

INSTEAD OF MOON

I can put chocolate, codeine
and even Valium suppositories
into the holes of receiving
I can hood a cloth lover
Reared by the wire one
with the glassed-over eyes
I too choose oblivion.

BACI

all things in equal measure
half in pain and half in pleasure

I OFTEN PRAY FOR THE PLANE TO CRASH

Not in heaven. Not on Earth.
Not counted as the living
Not among the dying either.
half dazed half numb

this pinioned kite.

we sit and pray the rosary of tiny creamers
it says half and half it says

I'm thinking *He is half poem, he is half stream.*
"I've seen trees cut right down the
middle, from roof to root,
carry on standing like a half-invisible man."

Liminal
As a child, I believed in goodness.
There was a side to take.
As an adult, I know it's complicated
and I don't care anymore.
We've taken all the great and
small minds of each generation
and applied them
to the Why and What, only to sing:
"Is that all there is?"
When it's been found out,
all of the time.
Most of it is pain.

I AM THE KING OF EPHYRA, DOGGED BITCH OF A WOMAN

In the night
I wake up looking for our love restored
You said *yeah I got swept up*
As though that's over now
Swept away these days, not off feet
Away—out towards the delta of estrangement
Under dirty carpets and
cheap motifs in hotel after hotel
in unread messages and missed calls

Swept away on thoughtless rafts
of *not really paying attention*

No one listening, I cannot rest
Somas in the hotel windows
Figures of longing arranged
in a tableau historical

I tossed away the gifts in anger
I toppled to erase my side of the mirror
I tippled with my begging cup
I called for oblivion

But even still I am a dog
checking the black window
for the return of my master,
your affections

It was summer then and winter now.
crumbs from off the icy mesa
fall inconsistently and without warning
Just enough to keep me seated at its meager base
faithfully waiting
and pathologically hopeful

Anxious, you call me,
Summing me Down
again to the foot
of your half-buried mountain
to clamber up once more
your facing back is sheer and cutting

veins show through the backs of my ugly hands
Shame shows through the backs of our ugly sheets

Nearing the peak I long to behold
you to be free of the bouldering task

You're always turning me into
the valley near the finish
I wonder if you cannot bear
the scarred breasts and woman flesh
which I too resent

But even face-down I climb you,
A would-be Sisyphus of love
You a silent Everest impassable

I'll try you again when I get home

QUOTING FROM TARKOVSKY'S *NOSTALGHIA*

cut the tongue of ingratitude
recall folk songs only
thank god from the dust of famine

“I don't want to take it alone.
All this beauty of yours”

women mourn and shear themselves
I mourn and let my graying hair grow long

TOO MUCH HEMINGWAY

In fallow fields long lived dust
the shape of future lovers
dedication to control and separateness,

They wore the clinging husks
Of an incomplete transformation
that inevitably left them behind

A city of devouring urges
corrupting elsewhere.

RECIPE FOR RESURRECTING A LOST LOVER

The back of a head in the palm
Rungs the ladder spine
Skate the line of the face
Butterfly kiss the spirit
See hands dance in conversation
Savor the favored eye
Does sleeping breath sound
The discovery of a word
One wrinkled smile
Curling tender child of night
A string of spent pearls
Come closer, ghost
Let me take in your neck
Whisper me a line
About carnations
Once more

IN BERLIN

I embrace strangers
Though I am a house of pain
There is always room for more
Their stones can be left in my body
So that they who come can be made lighter
My altar is broadened and a place for
Every foreign sadness is made here
Old ruins never really leave the flesh
A damaged liver
A humor forever unbalanced
Follicles deprived sacrifice their coppers
And creak out graying strands
One joint in the index finger protesting
No one mentioned giving up at all
It is in giving that we receive
I shall not seek to be consoled
From on the cold floor, a tree is seen.
Dead straight and tall and working
She grows beyond her confines
Neuralgia and the chaos of dying eyes
The skylight opens to other possibilities
Even in this small moment of escape;

I dreamed I loved you
I dreamed I owned you

ARS POETICA AS A WAY OF LIFE

Reading the same books for months,
you didn't ever seem to get through them.
I'd look over the titles
you carried through the trips and visits,
clocking that they largely remained the same.

From my industrious capital,
I'd glare down at you—
with your secret notes,
written with that special
pencil so thick and undainty—
At your keys and rituals.
Sigils in a society
of which I was not initiate, but tourist.
I thought it was fear
that imprisoned you in the pages.
Or procrastination.
Whatever kept you from any finishing.
You could linger in things.
You say poetry is a slow art
and that darkness is just darkness.

Eventually I realize that I am beneath it all.
Ignorance riding a high horse.
A tick on the high horse even.
I know nothing, it's true.
I've always wanted to get the day over with.
To leave the party early.
To get past everything
to where the end of suffering might lie,
just beyond the boundary of the predictable.

I think it's tomorrow

I xanned over months and years
and so never learned
and didn't develop any sophistication or resilience
and so have no immunity to your lingerings in me.

The problem with any experiential knowledge
is that it adds to what seems predictable
and therefore reports:
no further *attention* is required.
Yours was so refined and intoxicating.
It made me want to learn to stay in a day.

You are out there in California,
still savoring the pages and living within the lines,
themselves infinitely giving.
Unraveling the world, and me, this way
in one long unbroken curling skin.
Revealing of a beauty as it was written
by each sibling of your council,
within their pulpit frames.

You did also delight in the afternoon
sun dancing on the bathroom floor.
And could revel in an endless cup.
Then cook a meal for days.
Need little love for years
and remain fresh and sated.

This left me in ignorance of belonging
and a student of the snail
and of the hermit,
whom I'd mistaken for a hanged man.

You have your own light,
such brilliance.
Mine lume is
just darkness.

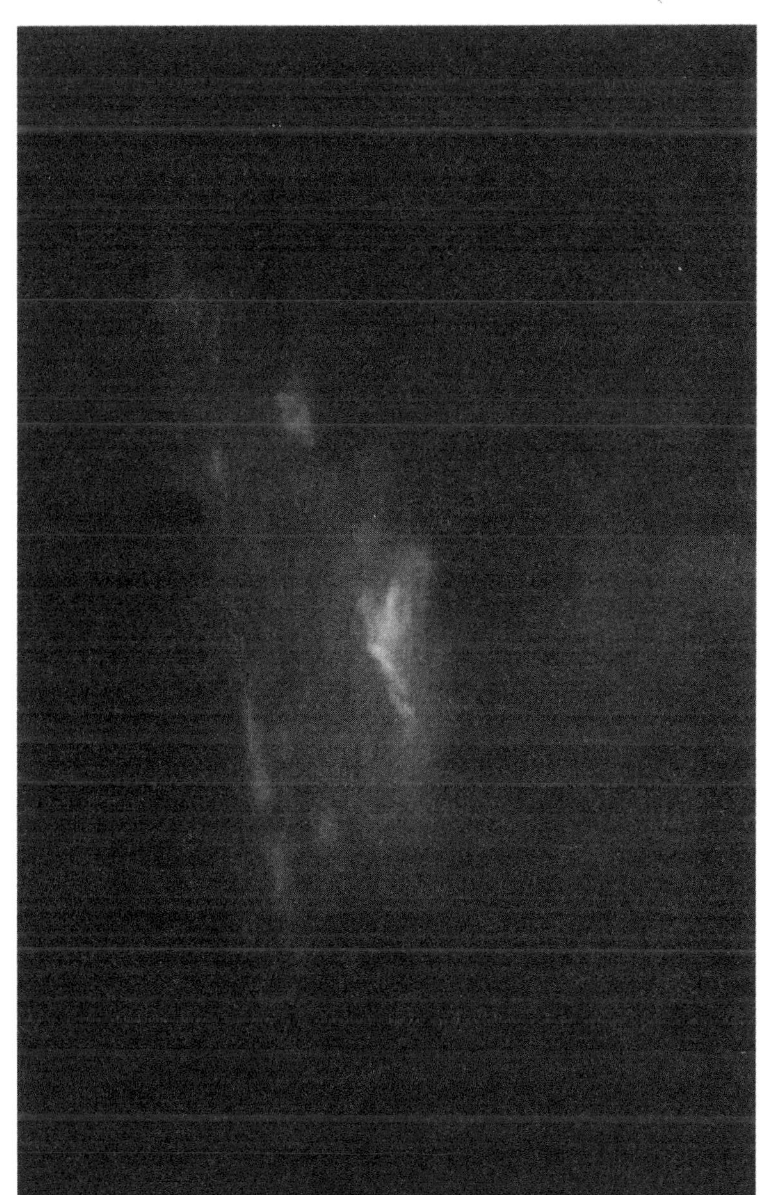

DERISION FEAT. DECORUM

Peak life is the moment before the anesthetic takes you blissing from
chore to door.
The last time you lay with your lover, knowing you'll never be able
to keep him.
Asking for the hospital chaplain's blessing before your womanhood
goes a-vivisecting.
Your children incinerated, are free from ever having to get born.

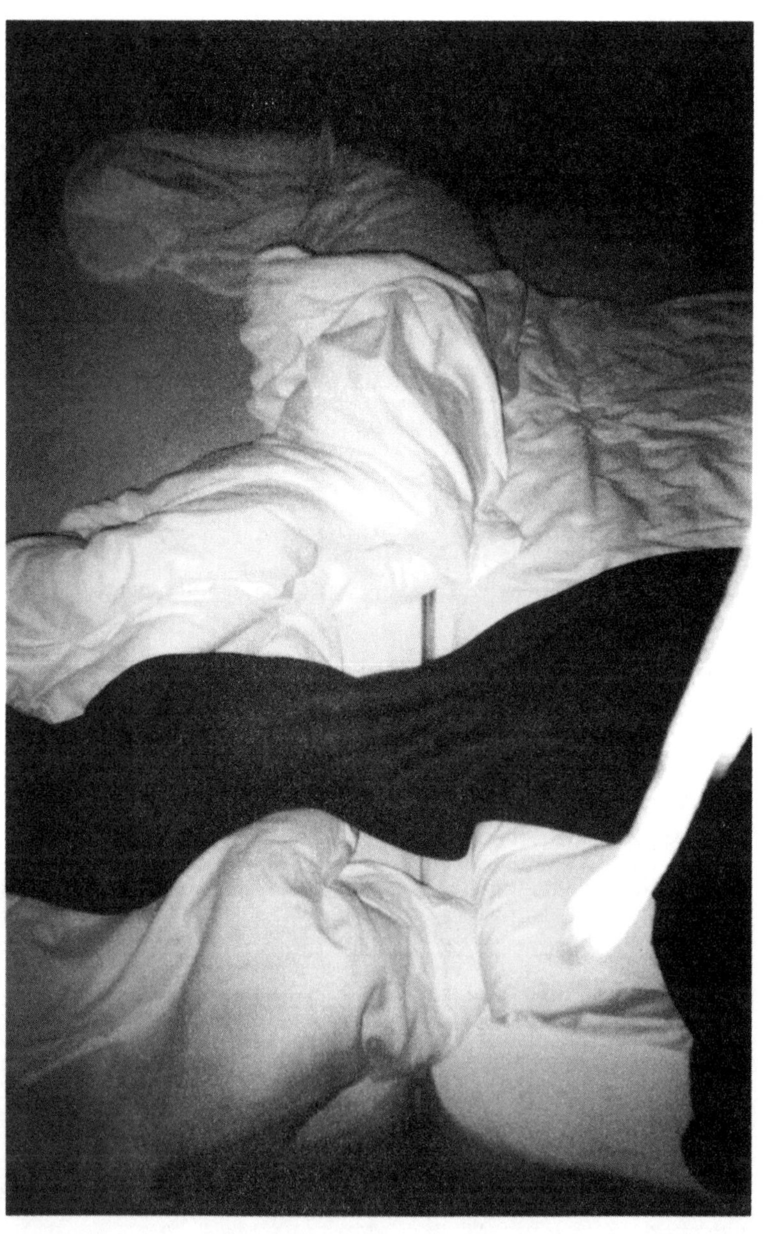

NATORI

Old black panties
made your day
So I bought new lacy ones
and even a matching bra
They came in the mail
a month or so too late
Now I carry them around the world with me,
unopened
Not enjoyed
At the bottom of a
suitcase along with three condoms
Hoping I'll run
into you by way of a stranger.

I dream of becoming a nun
and getting married to god
Black panties for black dress
Divorce my sex and rest
When we first met
my hand became alive
and sent to me all your
careful information
and I was touched
Sometimes I try to gesture in this

way in the odd hotel jet-lagged hue
Every time erupting in tears before it's over
And redact the moment I walked into a son
look for anyone to fill the void
But no one comes

BACI

Let it be known
I was not a woman
just a dickless bottom
hallowed by thy name

KITE, KNOWN AS HOPE

is in the shape of a person

who's bitter black horses painted wide and riding.
who is buoyant in a blind and perilous sky.

the mountain pours mountain down the clouds,
wondering at Man and His Symbols.

Who loosed the slack-jaw draping night only
to throw its handful fats under Daedalus's son?

I could see you were midair in this way...

and all around the high hall, tower
crumbles tower down the youngest
of the languages, leaving its condemned
men to hang in the wordless air.

IN CONVERSATION WITH THE ABYSS AS A PARISIAN

There is no more
Honey in the jar
Because I traded that gold
for coins
Tossed at my feet
on a stage in France
Without shoes I treaded the dais
And gave away the last of myself
To one stranger
on the left side of the front row
whose name I'll never learn

"Et quand ce fut fini, je t'ai pris dans mon évanouissement—
dissimulé dans des ténèbres scintillantes.
Ma robe autour de tes yeux et de ta voix"

Sugar is always the ask
Of my dizzy-making captor

"Sucre"

Together, We would drink
A spirit or a sweet thing

"Mais il n'y a pas de miel dans le pot"

But all the spirits abandoned place years ago
unbothered—in search of others to inspire
And now I'm in a hotel

with no feelings
And no sight
And no voice
And no swan

Showered like a loveless Danaë
After some precious meddle

ENTRY 17

Got lost of my self somewhere around number 10 entry
Foreignness stuffed into two repulsive legs
Looking downwards, they seemed ancient miles away
And the vast desert between them
The deadly desert.
The sink was settling and making a home in me at that time.
I began to taste:
of sand
of gray
of rank
of a salt crust left in the dry wash
(who'd seen 1000 flooding tears come and go)
of ketamine fizz
of a migrained palette and its kaleidoscoping auras
(moving like a mouthful of technicolor maggots)

of abandonment...

of menstrual blood left bleeding four days in the pad and pressed up
against the hot deadly desert
of the grim unwashed dogs having feasted on cat feces in the urban snow
of the sympathies piled high by the spirits haunting *my* house
of ant traps and cardboard boxes
of open mouth sleeping
of grandfather's death tallow of catheters
of extension cord rope swings

longing for a solid hang
languishing in the possibilities of the medicine cabinet

of VOCs and drying paint.

I couldn't paint
or play at that point
but I paid someone to come and do it all.

I failed to live in me.

So I rejoined the safety of the circus
And we traveled again together
Spinning the songs and singing for a small fee.
Remaking the safety needed by those
who might wish to weep in peace
Those who need to be carried on
the voice of a Jungian mother so that
they might feel their sufferings more precisely.

In every city and village
we pitch the chapel tent
we unfurl our wounded banner
And welcome the mourners
Crowds come for the beauty and spectacle of our solemnities
Night after night it went on this way

until I'd a l m o s t f o r g o t

a b a n d o n m e n t ' s   s i z e

It might have been years or days
before I arrived here, thinner
almost unrecognizable… I'm standing:

Under an olive tree at the Belevedere
with a man who cannot speak
The planets kissing at dusk
We watch.
The man shakes, but we do not kiss.

I want to find familiarity in him
I want to find home
That any one man
could be any man
could be you

They always bring me books
instead of love.

ABANDONMENT'S SIZE

pull book apart to reveal more of the dark inner seam.
Bring face to book, all the way to face, but not touching face,
while gazing into the seam.
imagine the event horizon of a black hole there.
try to look into it.
it never ends.
close the eyes and visualize the enveloping edge...
do not let the book rest on your face
(that would be a comforting thing to do.
you may linger here)

BACI

Bodies left unclaimed after 30 days outside the city limits
will shunt a passage between worlds

CAN HOPE TAKE THE SHAPE OF A PERSON?

I did wander into the son who would eventually become the Moon alone my loneliness interrupted I am, indeed, a Fool

MOON AS BOULDER FLOWN, DRIVEN, FERRIED, TRAINED, AND PUSHED TO THE FOLLOWING LOCATIONS TRAVELED THE FOLLOWING DISTANCES IN MILES

Portland /
f.7120 / Wellington / f.1383.19
/ Sydney / f.443.3 / Melbourne / f.466 / Hobart
/ f.8214 / Portland / f.5213 / Porto / d.194.48 / Lisbon /
d.91.96 / Leiria / d.115.57 / Porto / f.859 / Lille / d.354 / Rennes /
d.216.85 / Paris / d.305.71 / Strasbourg / d.106.1 / Dampierre-les-Bois /
d.321.29 / Brussels / d.34.17 / Ghent / d.131.73 / Nijmegen / d.395.12 /
Berlin / d.179.57 / Hamburg / d.246 / Leipzig / d.273.40 / Bochum / d.149.12
/ Wiesbaden / d.361.63 / Sion / d.612 / Amsterdam / f.5004 / Portland / f.5004 /
Amsterdam / f.112 / Brussels / d.370 / Birmingham / d.118 / Leeds / d.96 / Newcastle
/ d.151 / Glasgow / d+fr.142 / Belfast / d.227.5 / Limerick / d.124.89 / Dublin / d+fr.323 /
Bristol / d.177 / Manchester / d.218 / London / d.64.4 / Brighton / d.64.4 / London / f.4784.7 /
Seattle / f.129 / Portland / f.873 / Palm Springs / d.26 / Palm Desert / d.58 / Landers / d.58 /
Palm Desert / d.26 / Palm Springs / f.873 / Portland / f.5004 / Amsterdam / f.387.7 / Ålborg /
d.228 / Oslo / d+fr.595.8 / Espoo / d+fr.66.4 / Tallinn / d.121 / Riga / d.184.5 / Vilnius / d.324.9
/ Warsaw / d.180.1 / Kraków / d.169.6 / Wrocław / d.179.5 / Praha / f.442 / Amsterdam / f.5004
/ Portland / f.5004 / Amsterdam / d.116.1 / Groningen / d.146.6 / Den Haag / d.160.9 / Liège /
d.536 / Milano / d.133.59 / Bologna / d.88.8 / Verona / d.370.9 / Lyon / d.188.8 / Montpelier
/ d.268.4 / Pau / d.347.3 / Tours / d.336.7 / Brussels / f.713.59 / Rome / t.108 / Assisi /
t.108 / Rome / f.713.59 / Brussels / d.130.48 / Amsterdam / f.5004 / Portland / d.316 /
Vancouver / d.143 / Seattle / d.174 / Portland / d.635 / San Francisco / d.383 /
Los Angeles / f.1741 / Chicago / d.521 / Toronto / d.550 / Boston / d.216
/ New York / d.216 / Boston / f.4085.5 / Rome / t.108 / Assisi / f.721 /
Rotterdam / d.52 / Tilburg / f.75.8 / Amsterdam /
f.5004 / Portland / f.5004 / Amsterdam /
f.806.5 / Rome /t.108 /
Assisi

Camus is laughing; at least someone is.

FROM STRAWBERRY MOON TO STRAWBERRY MOON IN MILES

*

*

* Miles Flown 80,106.

z=^=>

*

()

(___)

^^^ ^^^^ ^^^ _____I_____ Miles

^^ Sailed 2,608

^^^^ ^^^^ __________/

^^ ^^ ^^ ^^^

150,800

_____

[()\

Miles Driven ============O———O========

============================

YOU INSTRUCTED ME TO WRITE THIS POEM, AND IT'S THE LAST ONE I'LL WRITE

"I love you in many ways," that was the rule for the first line.
Love, and it's not past tense one year on
Though it's mostly expressed in excruciations
And rarely, the shimmering joy

The blood-sequin coat of reversible relation
Alternately changing my skin,
Sometimes on the hour
I could be flayed as anything that hates
Then affectionately *thinking about* inside a dead animal

All the while
La Bella Vista's
felted hammerings
hobbled together a sense of us
for me to tether myself to

How a hotel pillow becomes you.
little seismic events
In my chest signaling
Ocular seas rising.
Dead Seas floating.
Boatless. Eyeless
Mouse me paddling hard

A year has passed between our strawberry moons
A June to June

and Sakamoto has died

We are still on the blue couch
Rigid in all the wrong ways.
Denim things. Starchy things.
Sleepy morning sticks piled in a happy heap

It's a shame about the armor
We dragged around
We didn't choose to be made,
And I didn't write this to remember.

Maybe I did it because I said I would
Maybe because I wanted to outrun you
Or twist the knife
Or speak to you in a language you could hear

Get up to your level somehow

To reach you, I guess
To touch the poet one more time.
Maybe because:
Even now:

Though you are not mine
I am yours, in me,
Even if it pushes you
And your little wooden heart away

I'm not sure if
I'm still mourning us,
Dressing in all this black,
Or trying to remain faithful
to The Lord of All Things

I carry in these clothes
A year ripped from the white hole in the night
called Moon
and suckle it from behind still skirts

I wonder if musicians writing poetry
is like actors starting bands...

It's not about being taken seriously,
anyway, you know.
It is about:
The Bella Vista

Soon these poems will
drift back into melodies...

Piano, piano
also means *softly, softly*

I'm not good at words
I'm not good at you
And I'm sorry for everything.

I think all artists crave to be sublimated
By their work
And the process, the time it requires

Maybe that's why our relationships
Are so fraught and puzzling
And hard to put down.
The best ones remain unsolvable

Maybe I asked too much of you,
looking back on it now.

In the year it's taken to write this,
having started it over many times.
From strawberry moon
To strawberry moon

I've been wearing us inside out.
But at least it's worn in now.

I don't think they tell you that
love is a reversible coat when they sell it to you

But I'm warm in a good way
And also fresh-faced
With Budd and Sakamoto
At *La Bella Vista*, and at *12*

Having learned the difference
Between loneliness
And aloneness

I'll always be
mixing up the medicine
You'll always be
mixing up the metaphors

Sakamoto breathes on
in my headphones
a bridge to a tenderness between you and me
a beauty so unkillable, so lasting

It's not something to get over, you see,
the rainbow, that is;

It's not just a trick of the light;
There is goodness in a man
In the ouroboral breath we share
In its iridescent sphere

and the split river smiles apart
a flowing silent at peace
the way a fleshy scar bows
into its surrounding skin

I can't know where all of this is taking you or me
I guess it's the not knowing which makes life worth living

It's that anything could happen
The way you happened out of thin air,
Out of the iridescent air,
In the moment I dropped my cane
and my guard

You appearing.

NOTES

Gratitude and acknowledgment is owed to Wesley Eisold for publishing in *Heartworm Reader*, vol. 2 (2023), earlier versions of the following poems: “At the Tomb of Saint Francis,” “The Starmaker,” “Flayed as Anything That Hates,” and “I Read Too Much Hemingway.”

In “Quoting from Tarkovsky’s *Nostalghia*,” “I don’t want to take it alone. / All this beauty of yours” is a quote from the 1983 film *Nostalghia* by Andrey Tarkovsky.

In “Flayed as Anything That Hates,” I pull in the line “*Non, je ne regrette rien*” from the eponymous song by Edith Piaf.

The title “Goodbye Horses” is taken from the song of the same name by Q Lazzarus.

“The Starmaker” is after the painting *Papilla Estelar (Star Maker)* by Remedios Varo.

And “The Bella Vista” is after the album *La Bella Vista* by Harold Budd—the inspiration for and emotional center of so much of this writing. I listened to this album more than six hundred times while writing the book. Thank you, Harold Budd.

ACKNOWLEDGMENTS

The cover photo is by the magical Ebru Yildiz, taken at the Hotel Chelsea during a truly special day together—thank you.

I want to thank the wonderful people at Unnamed Press who have given their time and attention to the creation of the book you hold in your hands. Chris Heiser, my editor, for his discerning eye and endlessly cool demeanor. Jaya Nicely, who carefully chose the fonts and slayed the cover and interior layouts. To Allison Miriam Smith, Cassidy Kuhle, Nancy Tan.

A special thank-you to Chad Luibl, whose enduring belief in storytelling and the arts gave me the opportunity to share mine. From a Zoom meeting during lockdown to standing on the terrace at J&N to eating tiramisu and talking about music. Thank you for believing in me.

To everyone else at J&N who worked on this book: Roma Panganiban, Michael Steger, Kian Maple, and Julia Quintos. Thank you.

To the compassionate friends, family, fellow travelers, and artistic collaborators who surrounded me and put up with my sad bullshit during the years of writing and beyond: Cintamani Calise, Marco Mazzola, Cedric Demolis, Jo Quail, William Fowler Collins, Patrick Shiroishi, Mason Rose, Marika Zorzi, Jesse Shreibman, Morgan May, Dave Elitch, Blake Armstrong, Becky Laverty, Sarah Lyon, Geert Braekers and Mark G., Sarah Ray Rundle, Liam Neighbors, and my faithful dog, Red.

Thank you to all the early readers of this work and to those who gave me their time, input, encouragement, and/or advice on writing and arranging poetry: Dylan Desmond, George Clarke, Hanif Abduraquib, Ioanna Gika, Kaveh Akbar, Sadie Dupuis, Meredith Graves, Peter Hughes.

Thank you to my manager, KW Campol, at Mythos Management for all that you do and to Ashley Craig at Mythos.

Thank you, sweet reader.

BACI

soul
cell
check
mate